Department of the Environment
Ancient Monuments and Historic Buildings

Rushton Triangular Lodge

NORTHAMPTONSHIRE

SIR GYLES ISHAM FSA

LONDON: HER MAJESTY'S STATIONERY OFFICE

First published 1970
Third impression 1975

ISBN 0 11 670061 0

Contents

Sir Thomas Tresham and his forbears

Sir Thomas Tresham (1545–1605) was the head of a family, well established in Northamptonshire since the early years of the fifteenth century. Coming originally from Gloucestershire, they took their name from an insignificant village near Wotton-under-Edge, in that county. William Tresham, who married Isabel, daughter of a Northampton lawyer William Vaux, was the first of the family to become prominent in national affairs. Through his marriage, he became allied to a family who in two generations had married heiresses and become rich and influential. William Tresham's brother-in-law, Sir William Vaux, was sheriff of Northamptonshire in 1436, and represented the county in Parliament in 1442. Tresham himself was twelve times MP for the county between 1423 and 1449, and four times elected Speaker of the Commons. He had probably inherited the manor of Sywell from his father, and in 1437 he purchased the manor of Rushton, henceforward the principal seat of the family. In 1450 he was murdered by the servants of Lord Grey of Ruthyn, for reasons that are obscure. His son, Thomas, was also wounded, but recovered to serve the House of Lancaster as his father had done, both as MP and Speaker of the Commons. Like his kinsmen, the Vauxs of Harrowden, this allegiance was to cost him dear, and after the Battle of Tewkesbury (1471) he was beheaded by order of the victorious Edward IV.

John Tresham, the son of Thomas, contented himself with country life. He built the house at Rushton, which still remains, in plan, as he made it, although there have been many alterations and rebuildings. John's son, another Thomas, was knighted by Henry VIII in 1530 and, like his grandfather, devoted himself to public affairs. He proclaimed Mary Tudor Queen at Northampton in 1553, and was made Lord Prior of the Order of St John of Jerusalem, when the Queen restored the Order, which her father had suppressed. His tomb may be seen in St Peter's Church at Rushton, wearing the dress of a Knight Hospitaller. He died in 1560, and his grandson, Thomas, then a boy of fifteen, succeeded to the large but scattered possessions of the Treshams, Thomas' father, John, having predeceased the Lord Prior. It has been said that Thomas had been brought up as a Protestant, and although this seems unlikely, Thomas must have conformed to the Elizabethan settlement, or he would never have been knighted, as he was, by Queen Elizabeth at Kenilworth Castle in 1570.

In 1580, however, he was reconciled to the "old religion" by the Jesuit missionary, Robert Parsons, and thereafter lived the life of a hostage, being imprisoned whenever the Government felt itself threatened from within or outside the kingdom. He spent fifteen years in prison, and paid in fines and penalties the enormous sum of £7717 12s od. Small wonder, then, that, in the words of Thomas Fuller: "Hard to say whether greater his delight, or skill in buildings, though more forward in beginning than finishing his fabricks."

SIR THOMAS TRESHAM'S BUILDINGS

First in date of his buildings was the Market-house at Rothwell, where Tresham was lord of the manor. The agreement with the mason, William Grumbold, is dated 1578 for "certaine workes to be done at Rothwell Crosse," which almost certainly refers to the Market-house. In 1583, Tresham thanked Sir Christopher Hatton for a gift of stone from his quarries at Weldon "for the finishing of Rothwell Cross," and this has generally been taken to refer to the Market-house, although it is not explained why it was apparently unfinished, and had to be roofed in in the nineteenth century. Possibly it was finished, and later despoiled. As a Latin inscription on the Market-house records, it was built "as a tribute to his sweet fatherland and County of Northampton, but chiefly to this town his near neighbour."

Other work undertaken by Tresham was alteration and addition to Rushton Hall in 1595, and extensive alteration, practically a rebuilding, of the manor house at Lyveden. Although much of the work at the old building, as it is now called, must date from after Tresham's death, and must be ascribed to his second son, Sir Lewis, Sir Thomas certainly began to work there, as is proved by an extant letter to his steward, dated 1604, referring to it. More important, from 1594, he became interested in a new building at Lyveden, a "Garden Lodge," surrounded by elaborate gardens. He was certainly engaged on this work in 1597, but progress was slow, partly because in 1599 he was back in the Fleet prison, although this time owing to a dispute over money with his son-in-law Fulcis, a former servant stigmatised by Sir Thomas as an "arrant varlet." This was not the end of his embarrassments, as he had to find £3000 to help his unstable son, Francis, who had rashly embroiled himself in Essex's conspiracy. Small wonder that the New Building was also left unfinished at Sir Thomas' death on 11 September 1605.

As soon as Sir Thomas was dead, the conspirators approached

View from the east

Francis Tresham to take part in the Gunpowder Plot. They hoped to use his considerable wealth and property, damaged as it was by his father's numerous fines and imprisonments. Francis had thought that the Plot "would not be the means to advance our religion but to overthrow it," but he allowed himself to be drawn in to the extent that he did not inform the Government of its existence, and was treated as a traitor, dying in the Tower of London as a prisoner.

It should be explained that Sir Thomas Tresham himself was considered by one of Cecil's informers "a very good subject and a great adversary of Spanish practices," and there is no reason to doubt his protestation that if the enemy had landed in England, he would have craved a place in the vanward of the battle "to witness to the world and leave record to all posterity of our religious loyalty and true English valour in defence of her sacred Majesty's person, and noble realm of England."

In 1619 the estate was bought by a London merchant, William Cockayne, and it remained with this family until 1828, thereafter passing through the families of Hope, Clarke-Thornhill and Pain.

In 1951 the Lodge was placed by Mr G. H. Pain of Great Glen Manor, Leicestershire, in the guardianship of the Ministry of Public Building and Works (now the Department of the Environment) under the provisions of the Ancient Monuments Acts.

The Triangular Lodge

This is the only extant complete work by Tresham. In plan, it is an equilateral triangle, with three storeys with three windows on each side on each floor; each side has three gables, rising to three tapering pinnacles. At the intersection of the roof is a three-sided chimney-stack. Below the gables is a frieze with a continuous inscription carried round the three sides, each side (33ft long) bearing 33 letters.

The building is thus symbolical of the Holy Trinity, and, as at Lyveden, the symbolism pervades every detail of the building. At Lyveden, the cross and passion of Christ are symbolised, closely linked with the sufferings of Our Lady. At Rushton, the doctrine of the Trinity is symbolised, but, with it, is linked the doctrine of the Mass. There is also intended an elaborate play on Tresham's own name, and his coat of arms, containing three trefoils. To modern ideas, of course, this punning seems a little out of place for such a solemn theme, but it is entirely in accord with much Elizabethan thought and poetry. Sir Thomas during his lengthy imprisonments made elaborate notes and sketches showing how his mind worked. Much of the heraldry of the period—deriving, of course, from the work of the medieval heralds—was of the "canting" or punning type. Shakespeare himself makes use of the heraldic pun even at solemn moments. "Now is he total gules" exclaims the first player in *Hamlet* to describe the blood-covered Priam.

The Triangular Lodge at Rushton is not the only Trinitarian building erected in Elizabethan times. Longford Castle in Wiltshire was finished in 1591 by Sir Thomas Gorges, and precedes Tresham's work at Rushton. Gorges' wife was a widow who had been the wife of William Parr, the Marquess of Northampton, a first cousin of Anne Parr, Tresham's grandmother. It can, therefore, be assumed that Tresham knew of Longford Castle and set out to imitate it after his own manner.

The building, of course, was not just a folly. The Rushton accounts invariably call it "The Warryners Lodge," and it was no doubt used by the keeper, who had charge of the rabbits, the keeping of which, like the pigeons in the dovecot, was a cherished prerogative of the lords of the manor and, we cannot doubt, equally irksome to their tenants.

THE SYMBOLISM EXPLAINED

Over the entrance door on the south-east front of the Lodge are the words TRES TESTIMONIUM DANT (There are three that bear witness) taken from the first epistle of St John. This is typical of the symbolism employed throughout the building. As the Authorised Version renders the passage ". . . there are three that bear record in heaven, the Father, the Word and the Holy Ghost: and these three are one."[1] This is the doctrine of the Holy Trinity to which the whole building "bears witness." It is also a play on the name Tresham. The name was pronounced "Traysam" and usually spelt Tressam or Tresame. Lady Tresham in her letters calls her husband sometimes "Good Tres." so the inscription also means "I ,Thomas Tresham bear witness." Similarly the trefoils in the coat of arms are a canting allusion to the name of Tresham and, no less, a symbol of the Blessed Trinity.

The building is, of course, three-sided and each side has a special allusion to one person of the Holy Trinity. As if to emphasise the unity of the three persons are the letters carried right round the building over each of the top windows, which, when read consecutively, read:

MENTES TUORUM VISITA
(Visit the minds of Thy people)

This, as Miss Jourdain[2] was the first to notice, is the second line of the Latin hymn to The Holy Ghost, the *Veni Creator.*

The entablature carries on each side a verse from the Bible.

South-east side

On the south-east, or entrance side:

APERIATUR TERRA ET GERMINET SALVATOREM
Let the Earth open and bring forth a Saviour

This is from Isaiah, Cap. XLV, v.8. The full verse reads "Rorate, caeli, desuper, et nubes pluant Justum; aperiatur terra et germinet Salvatorem, et justitia, oriatur simul; ego Dominus creavi eum" (Drop down ye heavens from above, and let the skies pour down righteousness; let the earth open, and let them bring forth salvation, and let righteousness spring up together: I the Lord have created it (Authorised Version: the Latin of the Vulgate implies a Saviour, rather than just Salvation). The emblems on this side, the seven-branched

[1]Since the time of Dr Bentley (about 1700) this verse has been considered by radical critics to be an interpolation or gloss.

[2]*Memorials of Old Northamptonshire*, edited by Alice Dryden, 1903.

candlestick, the seven eyes of God, all point, as Miss Jourdain noted, to the first person of the Trinity, God the Father.

North side

The north face bears the legend on the entablature:

> QUIS SEPARABIT NOS A CHARITATE CHRISTI
> Who shall separate us from the love of Christ?

This is from St Paul's Epistle to the Romans, Cap. VIII, v. 35. The rest of the verse is particularly applicable to Thomas Tresham, for St Paul goes on with his question "tribulatio? an angustia? an fames? an nuditas? an periculum? an persecutio? an gladius?" (Shall tribulation, or distresse, or persecution, or famine, or nakednesse, or peril, or sword?) Thomas Tresham knew almost as much about such things as Paul himself, and must often have read this chapter with its triumphant conclusion: "Nor height, nor depth, nor any other creature, shall be able to separate us from the love of God, which is in Christ Jesus our Lord."

On this face, too, the emblems, the Hen and Chickens[3] and the Pelican in her piety,[4] are expressive of the second person of the Trinity, God the Son.

South-west side

On the south-west front the legend reads:

> CONSIDERAVI OPERA TUA DOMINE ET EXPAVI
> I have considered thy works, O Lord, and been afraid

This is an expansion of Habakkuk, Cap. III, v.2, Domine audivi auditionem tuam et timui. The words consideravi, etc, follow timui in

[3]Matthew, Cap. XXIII, 37. Also there are nine chickens corresponding to Sir Thomas's own sons and daughters.

[4]The Pelican as a type of Christ, and especially of the Eucharist, is an old Christian idea. St Augustine wrote, "This bird has . . . a great likeness to the body of Christ, whose blood nourishes us." The Latin hymn of St Thomas Aquinas, *Adoro te devote, latens Deitas* employs this figure to describe Our Lord, *Pie Pellicane Jesu Domine*. This is no doubt the immediate source of Dante's *il nostro Pelicano* in Paradiso XXV, 113, cited by Miss Jourdain. In art, the pupils of Giotto were the first to make frequent use of the Pelican iconographically (A. P. Freitaz in *Encyclopedia Cattolica*, IX (1952), Col. 1088; for this reference the writer is indebted to Mr Colin Hardie).

The south-east front

The north front

The south-west front

the Tract from the Mass of Good Friday. Here the symbols, too, are suggestive of the third person of the Trinity; the Dove upon a serpent coiled about the globe, a hand issuing from a sun (Pentecostal fire).

The words on the central gables of each face read consecutively:

RESPICITE NON MIHI SOLI LABORAVI
Consider that I laboured not for myself only

This is from Ecclesiasticus, Cap. XXXIII, v. 18, and is clearly an allusion to the builder, who intended his work to teach others. He was not building solely for himself and his "Warryner."

A very striking feature of the building is the chimney. This too has emblems which are full of meaning. It is triangular in plan, and the top of the chimney is covered with Tresham trefoils—the Trinity and the builder again. Each face of the chimney has a date, 1595, when, according to the Rushton papers, the chimney was built. The emblems and words have a meaning, which seems to have escaped previous commentators. First, there is the entrance or south-east side. Here the emblem is the sacred monogram IHS with a cross above, and the three nails used on the cross below, enclosed in an octagon, signifying regeneration. The legend below is ESTO MIHI. This is a contraction of Psalm XXX, v. 4, ESTO MIHI IN DEUM PROTECTOREM, ET IN LOCUM REFUGII, UT SALVUM ME FACIAS (Authorised Version has Psalm 31, v. 2, "Be thou my strong rock, for an house of defence to save me." The Vulgate rendering is translated in the Knox Bible, "Be Thou my God and protector, my stronghold of defence, to save me from peril . . ." It is the Introit for Quinquagesima Sunday). It would seem that Tresham wished to incorporate the symbolism of the Mass, for which he had suffered so much, with that of the Trinity. The name of Jesus (the monogram on the Host), the cross, the nails symbolise the Holy Sacrifice of the Mass. The symbolism is further reinforced by the other faces of the chimney. On the north side is the emblem of the Lamb of God in a square (symbolising the four evangelists) with the word, ECCE, the first word of the sentence the priest speaks when giving communion at Mass to the faithful: "Ecce agnus dei, ecce qui tollis peccata mundi" (Behold the Lamb of God, behold Him who takes away the sins of the world). On the south-west side of the chimney, we find a Tau (T) cross within a chalice, enclosed in a pentagon, which usually signifies salvation. The Tau cross is mentioned in the inscription in verse on the Crucifixion in the Oratory at Rushton Hall: ECCE

SALUTIFERUM SIGNUM THAU NOBILE LIGNUM (Behold the salvation-bearing symbol THAU, the noble Tree of Life). The Greek T or tau also stands, of course, for Tresham. The legend word on this side of the chimney is SALUS, salvation, an obvious allusion to the words of the priest at Mass, just after he has eaten the Host, and before he drinks from the Chalice, calicem salutaris accipiam, I will take the chalice of salvation. Thus, we have on the chimney a complete homily on the Mass, with a reminder that its retention must involve suffering. One further piece of symbolism may be intended. As Mr Gotch noted, ". . . the chimney rises mysteriously from the middle of the building, and as there is no wall immediately beneath it, it becomes an interesting speculation as to how the chimney is carried, for the plain flat white-washed ceiling of the Top Floor hides everything above it." We now know from the Rushton papers that a cross beam of timber was specially made to carry the chimney (28 June 1595). The mystery of the chimney was intentional. It was symbolic of the Holy Mystery of the Mass, and the words spoken at the consecration of the Chalice, mysterium fidei. Finally, to complete the story of the symbolism of the Trinity linked with the Mass, the initial letters, incised on the breast above the pipes which drain the roof (themselves enriched by nine gargoyles), and on shields below each pipe on the soffit, give the sentence

> SANCTUS SANCTUS SANCTUS DOMINUS DEUS SABAOTH QUI ERAT ET QUI EST QUI VENTURUS EST
> Holy, Holy, Holy, Lord God of Sabaoth
> Which was and is and is to come

This, as Mr Gotch correctly pointed out, is from the Revelation, or Apocalypse, of St John, Cap. IV, v. 8, only, in the Bible, God is described as "omnipotens" not "Sabaoth." The reason is clear. Tresham was thinking of the end of the Preface, just before the Canon of the Mass begins, where the word is "Sabaoth."

Sir Thomas apologised for the fancifulness of his devices in that the harder a conceit is to find out, the more commendable it is "so long as (ytt being discovered) ytt be perspicuously to the purpose." This is certainly the case in the richness of the symbolism of the Triangular Lodge.

There is not space here to explore all the symbolism in the Lodge, particularly the vexed question of the numbers in figures with which

Sir Thomas adorned the building. Miss Jourdain suggested on the basis of a book, *Prognostication for the year of Our Lord LXXVI made . . .* by John Securis, dated Anno Mundi 5538, that the 55.55 over the door represents the date of the building AD 1593 (i.e. Creation 3962 BC–AD 1593). In a similar way, the other dates record, according to her, the Deluge, the Call of Abraham, the death of the Blessed Virgin Mary, the date of the Passion. Mrs Lomas in her introduction to the Rushton papers bases her interpretation on a memorandum by Sir Thomas at Ely in 1597, when he decorated the walls of his prison chamber with symbolical devices and texts, and monograms, avoiding anything like a crucifix, which would have been expunged by his Protestant gaolers. In these notes, there is nothing about the Triangular Lodge, but a good deal of light is shed on how his mind worked. As Mrs Lomas says "by addition, multiplication, the use of Greek and Hebrew letters as symbols of numbers, and other fantastic arrangements Sir Thomas could obtain almost any result he pleased."[5]

DATE OF CONSTRUCTION, AND MASONS EMPLOYED

The Lodge was begun on 28 July 1594 and finished on 29 September 1597, although the earliest date on the building is 1593. This was, however, the date at which Sir Thomas returned to Rushton from his *résidence forcée* in his own house at Hoxton. He had been absent from his home for twelve years, and had spent this time either in prison in the Fleet, house-arrest at Hoxton or prison at Ely. As soon as he got back to Rushton in April 1593, he began to plan the Triangular Lodge, the fruit of his meditations and study in divinity while in prison. Hence the date 1593 on the building, which is followed by his initials T T.

The Rushton papers contain details of the work done from 1593 to 1597, when it was finished. The Tyrells, who were regularly employed on Tresham's estate as masons, and did other work for him, seem to have done the bulk of the work on the Triangular Lodge. However, a very skilful mason, Parris, joined the workers in May 1594, and was paid forty-five shillings "in part of his bargain for working the scutcheons." The scutcheons at the Triangular Lodge were mostly those of Tresham's own family, and other families nearly allied in

[5]Historical Manuscripts Commission, *Var. Coll.*, volume III, page xliv.

marriage. It is probable that Parris also did some of the other very fine carving including the gargoyles, and it is indeed mentioned that he did the "crestes." There is a reference on 4 July 1595 to "Parris and his manne finishing three maydheads and beginning two falcons," and Parris was also employed on the chimney carving "finishinge the lambe, cup and inscription, and making three dates, on eche side of the chimney one." "Old Tyrrol" and his sons lived on the Rushton estate, but Parris was a skilled free-mason who came from elsewhere. The name suggests a Welsh origin (Ap Harris), but there was a Recusant family of this name at Pudding Norton, Norfolk. They were gentry, but it is possible that Parris, the mason, belonged to a junior branch of the family.

THE INTERIOR

By comparison with the colourful and ornate exterior, the interior of the Lodge is plain and simple. On each of the three floors is one large room, hexagonal in plan and taking up most of the available area, leaving only small triangular spaces in each corner. One such space contains the newel staircase and the others form small chambers or closets.

The entrance is on the south-east, at the head of a short flight of steps. It leads to a tiny lobby, which has a draw-bar for securing the outer door, and then to the principal room at this level. There are windows in three of its walls, each made up of twelve small circular lights grouped in trefoils around a central cross. One of the crosses has been later enlarged. The other walls are plain save for a composition on each of two rectangular panels flanking a central shield, that on the east wall bearing the arms of Tresham.

Below this room is the basement which is partly below ground and is reached by the newel staircase in the east corner. The rooms are dimly lit from small triangular-shaped windows and cannot have been used other than for storage. However, there is a similar arrangement of rectangular panels flanking a central shield on two of the walls of the large room.

On the top floor the main chamber has a fireplace which is the only one in the building, though the present cast-iron surround is nineteenth-century. The ingenious arrangements to carry the flue from the corner fireplace to the central chimney, and the massive timbers employed to support the central stack, are now exposed though originally these would have been above a plaster ceiling.

The windows in this room are composed of large and small triangles variously arranged. Two walls have raised panels, the central shield of one plain but the other bearing the Tresham arms impaled with those of Throckmorton. At the head of the stairs is another shield with Tresham trefoils.

Leading off the large upper chamber is a small closet behind the fireplace with no windows though to maintain symmetry "blind" windows have been provided externally. Also on this floor, in the remaining corner, is a small chamber with two windows. From this and from the main room one obtains a prospect over the park which, though separated now, originally ran up to and included this eccentric, extraordinarily personal and very pleasing little building.

ACKNOWLEDGEMENTS

Much of the material in this guide is derived from "Sir Thomas Tresham and his Buildings" by the same author, which appeared in volume LXV (Part II) of the *Reports and Papers of the Northamptonshire Antiquarian Society*, 1966.

The illustrations on pages 12, 13 and 14 are reproduced from Samuel Buck's original drawings of 1730, kindly lent by the author.

Printed in Scotland by Her Majesty's Stationery Office at HMSO Press, Edinburgh
Dd 289712 K26 7/75 (12458)